1

**IRS EXEMPT ORGANIZATIONS
COLLEGES AND UNIVERSITIES COMPLIANCE PROJECT**

Executive Summary of Final Report
(posted *April 25, 2013,* revised with highlighted changes on *May 2, 2013)*

The IRS is nearing the end of its multi-year project on tax-exempt colleges and universities. The Colleges and Universities Compliance Project was launched in 2008 with the distribution of detailed questionnaires to 400 randomly-selected colleges and universities. The IRS selected 34 of the 400 for examination because their questionnaire responses and Form 990 reporting indicated potential noncompliance in the areas of unrelated business income and executive compensation.

As exams were getting underway, the IRS released an Interim Report, presenting a preliminary overview of questionnaire responses. Now, with more than 90 percent of examinations completed, this Final Report provides additional analysis of the questionnaire responses and focuses on the examination results. Because colleges and universities were not randomly selected for examination, no assumptions should be drawn about the UBI and compensation practices of other colleges and universities based on the examination results.

Examination Highlights

Underreporting of Unrelated Business Taxable Income (UBTI)

Unrelated business income (UBI) is the income from a trade or business regularly conducted by an exempt organization and not substantially related to its exempt purpose. Unrelated business taxable income (UBTI) is the UBI that is taxable after deducting expenses directly connected to the trade or business. Because UBTI is calculated by totaling the UBI from all activities and subtracting the total allowable deductions, losses from one activity can offset profits from another. Examinations have resulted in:

- Increases to UBTI for 90% of colleges and universities examined totaling about $90 million;
- Over 180 changes to the amounts of UBTI reported by colleges and universities on Form 990-T; and
- Disallowance of more than $170 million in losses and Net Operating Losses (NOLs, i.e., losses reported in one year that are used to offset profits in other years), which could amount to more than $60 million in assessed taxes.

The primary reasons for increases to UBTI in the completed exams were:

- *Disallowing expenses that were not connected to unrelated business activities:* The IRS found that examined colleges and universities were reporting certain losses as connected to unrelated business activities when they were not. The misreporting occurred in two ways:

    o *Lack of profit motive*: The IRS found that organizations were claiming losses from activities that did not qualify as a trade or business. Nearly 70 percent of examined colleges and universities reported losses from activities for which expenses had consistently exceeded UBI for many years. UBI must be generated by a "trade or business." An activity qualifies as a "trade or business" only if, among other things, the taxpayer engaged in the activity with the intent to make a profit. A pattern of recurring losses indicates a lack of profit motive. The IRS disallowed reporting of activities for which the taxpayer failed to show a profit motive. Those losses no longer offset profits from other activities in the current year or in future years, with more than $150 million of NOLs disallowed.

    o *Improper expense allocation:* The IRS also found that on nearly 60% of the Form 990-Ts we examined, colleges and universities had misallocated expenses to offset UBI for specific activities. Organizations may allocate expenses that are used to carry on both exempt and unrelated business activities, but they must do so on a reasonable basis and the expenses offsetting UBI must be directly connected to the UBI activities. In many cases, the IRS found that claimed expenses, which generated losses, were not connected to the unrelated business activity.

- *Errors in computation or substantiation:* The IRS checked the calculations for all NOLs reported on returns under exam and found that NOLs were either improperly calculated or unsubstantiated on more than a third of returns. As a result, the IRS disallowed nearly $19 million in NOLs.

- *Reclassifying exempt activities as unrelated*: The IRS determined that nearly 40 percent of colleges and universities examined had misclassified certain activities as exempt or otherwise not reportable on Form 990-T. Fewer than 20 percent of these activities generated a loss. The examinations resulted in the reclassification of nearly $4 million in income as unrelated, subjecting those activities to tax.

Examinations resulted in more than 180 changes to UBTI reported for specific activities by colleges and universities. More than 30 different activities were connected to the changes. The majority of these adjustments came from the following activities:

- Fitness, recreation centers and sports camps
- Advertising
- Facility rentals
- Arenas, and
- Golf

Compensation and Comparability Data

The executive compensation component of the examinations focused mainly on compliance with section 4958 of the Code, which provides that organizations may pay no more than reasonable compensation to their disqualified persons. Section 4958 applies to private, but not public, colleges and universities, and imposes an excise tax on disqualified persons who received payment of unreasonable compensation and on those persons who approved it. At the private colleges and universities examined, the officers, directors, trustees and key employees (ODTKEs) were disqualified persons subject to the reasonable compensation requirements of section 4958.

An organization may shift the burden of proving unreasonable compensation to the IRS by following the three steps of the rebuttable presumption process:

- Using an independent body to review and determine the amount of compensation;
- Relying on appropriate comparability data to set the compensation amount; and
- Contemporaneously documenting the compensation-setting process.

Although most private colleges and universities examined attempted to meet the rebuttable presumption standard, about 20% of them failed to do so because of problems with their comparability data including:

- Institutions that were not similarly situated to the school relying on the data, based on at least one of the following factors: location, endowment size, revenues, total net assets, number of students, and selectivity;
- Compensation studies neither documented the selection criteria for the schools included nor explained why those schools were deemed comparable to the school relying on the study.
- Compensation surveys that did not specify whether amounts reported included only salary or included total other types of compensation, as required by section 4958.

Compensation Amounts

Officers, Directors, Trustees and Key Employees (ODTKEs)

With few exceptions, each college or university examined identified its "top management official," who was usually the president, as its highest paid ODTKE. Overall, the average and median base salary and total compensation for the top management official of the colleges and universities examined, both public and private, were as follows:

- Average base salary: $452,883; median base salary, $376,018.
- Average total compensation: $623,267; median total compensation, $499,527.

Highly Compensated Non-ODTKEs

Although examinations focused on ODTKEs, the IRS also looked at compensation levels for most highly compensated non-ODTKEs. The most highly-paid non-ODTKEs fell primarily into one of five categories: Sports Coaches, Investment Managers, Head of Departments, Faculty and Administrative/Managerial. As shown below, Sports Coaches and Investment Managers received the highest average compensation at the colleges and universities examined.

Position	Average compensation
Investment Managers	$894,214
Sports Coaches	$884,746

Compensation amounts for non-ODTKEs in the remaining categories differed based on whether or not the non-ODTKE was a medical doctor. The second column below excludes the compensation paid to medical doctors, who comprise 30% of the ODTKEs reported in the first column. The most highly-paid non-ODTKE positions were as follows:

Position	Average compensation	Average compensation (excluding M.D.s)
Heads of departments	$753,738	$279,770
Faculty	$575,632	$215,854
Administrative/Managerial	$462,872	$381,745

Employment Tax and Retirement Plans

In addition to examining Forms 990 and 990-T focusing on UBI and compensation, the IRS also reviewed employment tax and employee plan returns. These reviews covered employment tax and employee plan issues for all employees, not just for ODKTEs and the highest-paid non-ODTKEs.

Employment Tax Issues

- The IRS looked at employment tax returns at about a third of the colleges and universities examined.
- All of the completed exams have resulted in adjustments in wages, and leading to assessment of tax and, in some cases, penalties.
- Wage adjustments total about $36 million, while taxes and penalties amount to over $7 million.

Retirement Plan Issues

- The IRS looked at retirement plan reporting at about a quarter of the colleges and universities we examined, and found problems at about half. These examinations have resulted in increases in wages of more than $1 million and the assessment of more than $200,000 in taxes and penalties.

Next Steps

The examinations of college and universities identified some significant issues with respect to both UBI and compensation that may well be present elsewhere across the tax-exempt sector. As a result, the IRS plans to look at UBI reporting more broadly, especially at recurring losses and the allocation of expenses, and to ensure, through education and examinations, that tax-exempt organizations are aware of the importance of using appropriate comparability data when setting compensation.

INTRODUCTION

This is the Final Report of the Colleges and Universities Compliance Project. The Exempt Organizations Division of the Internal Revenue Service (IRS) Tax Exempt and Government Entities Division launched the project in 2008 so that the IRS and other stakeholders could better understand tax-exempt colleges and universities and their practices involving endowments, executive compensation and unrelated business activities. This report is based on the responses to Questionnaires the IRS sent to a sample of 400 colleges and universities and on the results of examinations of 34 colleges and universities.

The IRS presented a preliminary look at project results in May, 2010, with the release of an interim report summarizing how small, medium and large institutions responded to much of the Questionnaire.[1] The Final Report provides a comprehensive view of what the IRS has learned from both Questionnaire responses and examinations. The report presents new information based on deeper statistical analysis of data presented in the Interim Report and on analysis of those Questionnaire responses that were not included in the Interim Report. Schools are not categorized by size in much of the Final Report. Instead, the analysis represents the colleges and universities sector as a whole, and as categorized by whether an institution is public or private, regardless of size. The Final Report also includes findings from the examinations of colleges and universities. In addition, appendices to the Final Report incorporate the Interim Report and the Questionnaire so that readers will be able to access all information on the project in one location.

I.   Key Differences Between the Interim Report and the Final Report

A. Examinations

Based on the responses to the Questionnaires and information on the Form 990, EO opened examinations of 34 colleges and universities. The examinations were designed to focus on unrelated business income and executive compensation. When the Interim Report was published, examinations were in their early stages. Now, with nearly all examinations closed, the Final Report includes a summary of what the IRS has learned from the examinations of colleges and universities.

B. Additional Data Analysis

The Interim Report described how three groups—small, medium and large colleges and universities—responded to much of the Questionnaire. To provide a more

---

[1] Interim Report on the IRS Exempt Organizations Colleges and Universities Compliance Project, May, 2010. See Appendix B.

comprehensive picture of the sector, for the Final Report, the IRS weighted data included in the Interim Report so that many of the findings could be extrapolated to apply to all tax-exempt colleges and universities and to private and public institutions as well. In addition to describing results in terms of the entire college and university sector (as opposed to small and medium and large schools within the sector), the Final Report incorporates information gathered from review of narrative responses to certain questions[2] that were not included in the Interim Report. It also includes, where possible, data generated through further analysis of questions that were included in the Interim Report.[3] Additional Data Analysis is in Appendix C.

C. Systems

The Interim Report did not include a discussion of responses submitted by colleges and universities that responded on a system-wide basis (rather than on a campus-only basis). The Questionnaire allowed system-wide reporting if (1) it was consistent with reporting on Forms 990 and 990-T and (2) the same method was used for all parts of the Questionnaire.[4] Information on the six systems that reported for 16 colleges and universities is included in Appendix D.

II.   Limitations of the Data

This report presents a broad picture of what is happening in the tax-exempt colleges and universities sector based on information gathered from Questionnaire responses and examinations. In presenting this information, the IRS has been careful to point out its limits. For example, in the Interim Report, the data applies only to categories of universities based on their size—small, medium, or large--but cannot be used to draw conclusions about all colleges and universities or the typical college or university. Building on what was included in the Interim Report, much of the data in the Additional Data Analysis has been weighted so that it can be extrapolated to give a sense of the characteristics, activities and tax reporting of colleges and universities overall—and of public and private colleges and universities overall—regardless of size.

Some of the data in the Additional Data Analysis, however, has not been weighted to produce one overall result. Much of the compensation data, for example, applies to

---

[2] This includes Questions 21, 24, 25, 29, 57, 76 and 79. The IRS reviewed narrative responses to all questions and, where possible, presented a summary of those responses in the Additional Data Analysis.

[3] This includes Questions 17, 23, 27, 56, 60 and 80.

[4] This issue and several others related to completion of the Questionnaire (including an extension of time for completion) were addressed in "Questions and Answers," which is included at the end of the Questionnaire in Appendix A.

individuals within colleges and universities. Weighting of the college and university responses produced meaningful results at the entity level, but not when broken down to data about individuals within entities. Similarly, narrative responses included a great deal of variation. The integrity of those responses could be maintained when summarized by size of school, but would have been lost if weighted and extrapolated across size-based categories to "average" narrative responses. Therefore, the report notes when data applies to all colleges and universities (or to public or private colleges and universities) and when it can only be applied to the schools that fall within the small, medium and large size-based categories. In addition, the IRS did not confirm the accuracy of answers to Questionnaires. The IRS analyzed and reported whatever the respondents reported and did not reconcile Questionnaire responses against Form 990 reporting or examination findings. Agents did, of course, use Questionnaire responses to help inform their examinations, although most Questionnaire data reflects the 2006 tax year, and examinations represent a range of tax years primarily from 2006 to 2008.

EXAMINATION RESULTS

I.   Background

Examinations focused on compliance with the tax rules concerning unrelated business income (UBI) and compensation.

In selecting colleges and universities for examination, the IRS first reviewed Questionnaire responses to identify those respondents having the greatest potential for compliance issues with respect to UBI or compensation. The IRS then evaluated Form 990 reporting to further inform its selection process. In the end, the IRS chose 34 colleges and universities for examination, about equally divided between private and public institutions.[5]   About two thirds were large, with 15,000 or more students.

Examinations covered all returns related to the college or university under exam, including Forms 990 and 990-T and employee plans returns, excise tax returns and employment tax returns. EO drew on expertise from across the IRS to support the examinations. Federal, State and Local Governments (FSLG) participated in the examination of employment tax issues at state colleges and universities. Large Business and International (LB&I) supported the examinations by providing Computer Audit Specialists trained to handle the volume and complexity of accounting records produced by automated data processing systems. LB&I also provided Engineers to offer expert valuation of compensation at private colleges and universities. Finally, Wage and Investment (W&I) provided Employment Tax Specialists for selected private college and university examinations. On all issues, EO Examinations teams worked closely with Chief Counsel and with EO Rulings and Agreements staff.

Reporting the results of these examinations involves descriptions of the practices of the 34 selected colleges and universities with respect to UBI and compensation. These institutions were selected for examination because their returns and questionnaires indicated potential noncompliance in these areas. They are not a representative sample of all colleges and universities, and readers should not make assumptions about the UBI and compensation practices of other colleges and universities based on these examination results.

II.   Unrelated Business Income

As tax-exempt organizations, colleges and universities are not taxed on income from activities that are substantially related to their exempt purpose even if the activity is a trade or business. To be substantially related, activities must contribute importantly to the accomplishment of an organization's exempt purposes.

---

[5] 41 percent of 990-Ts examined reported UBI on a system-wide basis.

A college or university is subject to tax on income from an unrelated trade or business.[6] A trade or business is unrelated if it is not substantially related to the accomplishment of an organization's exempt purposes, even if funds from the business are used to support those purposes.[7]

Not all unrelated business income (UBI), however, is subject to tax. The law provides various exceptions and modifications to the calculation of unrelated business income tax (UBIT). Section 512 of the Code sets forth the rules for determining whether UBI is taxed, excluding income from certain types of activities[8] and also permitting all deductions directly connected with the unrelated trade or business. (Unrelated Business Taxable Income (UBTI) is the amount of UBI that is taxable after deducting expenses directly connected to the trade or business.

Many organizations generate UBI but pay no tax on that income.[9] The amount of UBI that goes untaxed each year is significant. In the examinations of colleges and universities, the IRS focused on how organizations report their business activities including the characterization of activities as exempt or unrelated, the methodology for allocating expenses, the significance of recurring losses on specific activities, the calculation of net operating losses (NOLs) and the application of exceptions and modifications. The IRS looked at these issues, and others, as they applied to a wide variety of activities including advertising and exclusive provider arrangements, sports management agreements, facility rentals, arenas, food service, golf courses, hotels, recreation centers and programs, parking lots, commercial research, and bookstores.

A. Activities and Changes to UBTI

The exams of 90 percent of colleges and universities ended with increases to UBTI. This includes more than 180 adjustments totaling about $90 million.

The activities below, in order of frequency, were connected to more than half of the adjustments:

---

[6] The unrelated business income tax applies to organizations that are exempt from income tax under section 501(a), which includes private colleges and universities. Section 511(a)(2)(B) provides that the tax applies to any state college or university or any corporation wholly owned by a state college or university.

[7] I.R.C. §513(a).

[8] I.R.C. §512(b). For example, dividends, interest, certain investment income, royalties, certain rental income, certain income from research activities, and gains or losses from the disposition of property are excluded when computing unrelated business taxable income (UBTI).

[9] Jael Jackson, "Unrelated Business Income Tax Returns, 2008," Sol Bulletin, Winter 2012. After reducing their gross unrelated business income by allowable deductions, only about half of all organizations that were required to file Form 990-T for Tax Year 2008 reported unrelated business income tax liability.

- Fitness and recreation centers and sports camps;
- Advertising ;
- Facility rentals;
- Arenas; and
- Golf courses.

Adjustments to UBTI generated by these activities affected a significant number of colleges and universities examined.

- Advertising and Facility Rentals resulted in changes in UBTI for nearly half of colleges and universities examined; and
- Fitness and recreation centers and sports camps, Arenas, and Golf courses resulted in UBTI adjustments for about a third of colleges and universities examined;

The IRS disallowed losses on 75 percent of returns examined. In total, the IRS disallowed more than $170 million in losses and Net Operating Losses (NOLs), which could amount to more than $60 million in assessed taxes. If an organization cannot use all of its losses to offset gains in a single tax year, it receives NOLs. It may carry over these NOLs for use going back two years and going forward for 20 years.

B. Reasons for adjustments

1. Misclassification as a Trade or Business: Lack of Profit Motive

A taxpayer can only generate UBI from a "trade or business." An activity qualifies as a "trade or business" if, among other things, the taxpayer engaged in the activity with the intention of making a profit. A pattern of repeated losses is generally sufficient to show a lack of profit motive. Continuous losses sustained beyond the period which is necessary to bring the operation to profitable status that are not due to customary business risks or reverses indicate that the activity is not operated as a trade or business being engaged in for profit. When income is attributable to an activity lacking a profit motive, a loss from the activity cannot be claimed on Form 990-T.

The most common reason, by far, for disallowance of losses and NOLs in the college and university exams was that claimed losses were connected with an activity for which the school lacked a profit motive, as evidenced by years of sustained losses. The IRS disallowed losses and NOLs for lack of profit motive at 70 percent of colleges and universities examined. These disallowances amounted to more than $150 million of the total losses and NOLs disallowed in the college and university exams.

Losses from a single activity can offset gains from other activities both in the year of the loss and in future and past years. UBTI is determined by subtracting from gross UBI all deductions directly connected with the unrelated trade or business.[10] If an organization carries on multiple unrelated business activities, its UBTI is the aggregate of its gross income from such activities minus the aggregate deductions.[11] An unrelated business activity that generates sufficient deductions may operate at a loss, which offsets not only the income from that activity but also gains from other unrelated business activities.

2. Misallocation of expenses

When a trade or business activity serves both exempt and unrelated purposes, the income and expenses from the activity must be allocated between the two on a reasonable basis.[12] Allocated expenses must have a proximate and primary relationship to the activities to which they are attributed. Only the expenses allocated to an unrelated trade or business are allowable as a deduction against UBI. Expenses attributable to accomplishing an organization's exempt purpose may not be deducted because the organization is already exempt from paying tax on related income.

Expense deductions were disallowed on more than 60 percent of Form 990-Ts examined because they were based on improper allocations between exempt and unrelated business activities.

3. Errors in computation or substantiation

The IRS checked the calculations for all NOLs reported on returns under exam and found that on more than a third of returns examined NOLs were either improperly calculated or unsubstantiated. As a result, the IRS disallowed more than $19 million in NOLs.

4. Misclassification of Related Activities

The IRS looked at activities that were not reported on Form 990-T to determine whether they were properly omitted. Activities that are substantially related to an organization's exempt purpose are not reported on Form 990-T. Likewise, certain income is specifically excluded from Form 990-T reporting. When activities are not reported on Form 990-T, they are effectively treated as if they are related activities. Income from related activities is not subject to tax.

At more than 40 percent of colleges and universities examined, activities that were effectively treated as related were determined, upon examination, to be unrelated activities that should have been reported on Form 990-T, and were subject to tax. These adjustments totaled nearly $4 million. Less than 20 percent of these activities generated a loss.

---

[10] IRC § 512(a).

[11] Treas. Reg. § 1.512(a)–1(a).

[12] Treas. Reg. § 1.512(a)–1(c).

5. Review of UBI Reporting

The IRS was interested in whether colleges and universities sought advice or review beyond their own professional staffs on UBI-related matters.

The IRS found that about 20 percent of colleges and universities examined sought outside advice about the tax treatment of specific potentially unrelated business activities. In about 40 percent of those cases where an institution had obtained an outside opinion, the IRS did not agree with the opinion when the issue came up on examination. For example, based on outside advice, the college or university might have treated an activity as related to its exempt purpose, but the examination resulted in reclassifying that activity as unrelated.

Of Form 990-Ts filed with the IRS by examined colleges and universities:

- 13 percent were reviewed by outside counsel before they were filed with the IRS.
- 57 percent were reviewed by independent accountants before they were filed with the IRS.
- Half of Form 990-Ts were reviewed before filing by the board of directors or a board committee.

III.   *Compensation*

The executive compensation component of the examinations focused on compliance with Section 4958 of the Code, which applies to organizations exempt from tax under section 501(a) and described under sections 501(c)(3) or 501(c)(4). This includes the private colleges and universities selected for exam. Section 4958 generally does not apply to public colleges and universities,[13] and they are not included in the Examinations section on Reasonableness of Compensation.[14]

---

[13] The income of public colleges and universities is generally exempt under section 115 because they are considered governmental units or affiliates. Some of these organizations still seek IRS recognition that they are also exempt under section 501(c)(3). In that case, they are exempted from section 4958 because they are not required to file an annual return because of their status as a governmental unit or affiliate. Treas. Reg. § 53.4958-2(a)(2)(ii).

[14] However, the IRS did gather information about compensation amounts and practices at public colleges and universities, so they are included in the other three sections: Compensation Amounts, Compensation-Related Adjustments and How Compensation Was Determined.

Section 4958 imposes an excise tax on compensation that constitutes an excess benefit transaction. An excess benefit transaction occurs when a disqualified person[15] receives more than reasonable compensation for services rendered to the organization. This report uses the terms, "Officers, Directors, Trustees and Key Employees," or "ODTKEs" to describe disqualified persons at the private colleges and universities examined. Reasonable compensation is understood to be the amount that would ordinarily be paid for like services by a like enterprise under like circumstances. In determining the reasonableness of compensation, all items of compensation are taken into account.[16]

The regulations under section 4958 set forth a process by which organizations can obtain a rebuttable presumption that compensation paid is reasonable.[17] In previous studies,[18] the IRS focused on the process by which organizations set compensation to see whether they were following practices that were consistent with meeting the rebuttable presumption of reasonableness.

During the examinations of colleges and universities, the IRS also enlisted the aid of LB&I Engineers to look behind the process and evaluate the comparability data relied upon in establishing the rebuttable presumption.

---

[15] Section 4958(f)(1) defines disqualified person, in part, as any person who was in a position to exercise substantial influence over the affairs of an applicable tax-exempt organization. Any person who holds any of the following powers, responsibilities, or interests is in a position to exercise substantial influence over the affairs of an applicable tax-exempt organization: (1) Voting members of the governing body; (2) Presidents, chief executive officers, or chief operating officers; (3) Treasurers and chief financial officers.

[16] Treas. Reg. § 53.4958-4. These include: All forms of cash and non-cash compensation, including salary, fees, bonuses, severance payments, and deferred and noncash compensation; The payment of liability insurance premiums, or the payment or reimbursement by the organization of taxes or certain expenses under section 4958, unless excludable from income as a de minimis fringe benefit ; All other compensatory benefits, whether or not included in gross income for income tax purposes; Taxable and nontaxable fringe benefits, except fringe benefits described in section 132; and Foregone interest on loans.

[17] Section 53.4958-6 of the regulations details this three-part process: (1) an independent body to review and establish the amount of compensation in advance of actual payment, (2) use of permissible comparability data to establish the compensation, and (3) contemporaneous documentation of the process used to establish the compensation amount. Compensation set pursuant to a process that satisfies these requirements is presumed to be reasonable in amount, and the IRS has the burden of proving that the compensation is excessive under section 4958. If the requirements are not met, the organization has the burden of proving reasonableness.

[18] In 2007, the IRS released a report on the Executive Compensation Compliance Initiative, and in 2009, the IRS released a report on the Hospital Compliance Project which included examinations of 20 hospitals focusing on executive compensation.

The sections below discuss what the IRS has learned about the amounts of compensation paid by the colleges and universities examined, the process by which those compensation amounts were determined, and whether those amounts were reasonable.

A. Compensation Amounts

1. Compensation paid to top management officials

The IRS looked at the compensation paid to Officers, Directors, Trustees and Key Employees (ODTKEs) at both public and private colleges and universities. With very few exceptions, the highest paid ODTKE at the colleges and universities examined was the individual identified as the institution's "top management official." In 80 percent of cases, that individual was described as the president or chancellor.

Average and median base salaries for the top management official of the colleges and universities examined were as follows:

Top Management Official – Base Salary		
	Mean	Median
Large	$461,332	$386,503
Medium	$419,925	$392,000
Small	$459,085	$294,479
Overall	$452,883	$376,018

Average and median total compensation for the top management official of the colleges and universities examined were as follows:

Top Management Official – Total Compensation		
	Mean	Median
Large	$661,706	$502,000
Medium	$551,656	$519,226
Small	$573,156	$379,029
Overall	$623,267	$499,527

2. Compensation paid to non-ODTKEs

The examinations also looked at amounts paid to highly-compensated individuals who are not ODTKEs. These non-ODTKES, by definition, are not disqualified persons covered by section 4958.

The information below describes the compensation for the individuals who were among the six highest-paid non-ODTKEs at each of the colleges and universities with closed examinations. (In other words, the numbers below represent about 180 individual non-ODTKEs employed by public and private colleges and universities.)

In order of highest to lowest average compensation by position:[19]

- Investment Managers
  - Investment Managers earned the highest average compensation, $894,214, with median compensation of $838,508.
  - 2 percent of the highest paid non-ODTKEs served primarily as Investment Managers.

- Sports Coaches
  - Sports Coaches earned the second highest average compensation, $884,746, with median compensation of $523,906.
  - 20 percent of the highest paid non-ODTKEs served primarily as Sports Coaches.

- Heads of departments
  - Heads of departments earned the third highest average compensation, $753,738, with median compensation of $654,451.
  - 16 percent of the highest paid non-ODTKEs served primarily as Heads of Departments.

- Faculty
  - Faculty earned the fourth highest average compensation, $575,632, with a median of $340,153.
  - 34 percent of the highest paid non-ODTKEs served primarily as Faculty (instructional and research).

- Other
  - Individuals in Other positions earned the fifth highest average compensation, $539,240, with median compensation of $476,665.

---

[19] Positions were counted in one of six categories: Faculty (Instructional and Research), Heads of Departments, Sports Coach, Administrative/Managerial, Investment Manager, and Other.

o About 6 percent of the highest paid non-ODTKEs served primarily in a category of position other than the categories listed above.

- Administrative/Managerial
  o Individuals in Administrative/Managerial positions earned the sixth highest average compensation, $462,872, with median compensation of $356,522.
  o 23 percent of the highest paid non-ODTKEs served primarily in Administrative/Managerial positions.

3. Impact of medical school positions

Some of the examinations covered undergraduate schools, graduate schools and professional schools. About 30 percent of the individuals who were reported as one of the six highest-paid non-ODTKEs were medical school faculty. They are included in three categories above: Faculty, Heads of Departments and Administrative/Managerial. Removing those individuals from the calculation substantially decreases the average, median and highest compensation amounts for each position.

- Heads of departments (not including department heads at medical schools)
  o Heads of departments earn average compensation of $279,770, with median compensation of $233,130.

- Faculty (not including medical school faculty)
  o Faculty earns average compensation of $215,854, with a median of $163,176.

- Administrative/Managerial (not including medical school positions)
  o Individuals in Administrative/Managerial positions earn average compensation of $381,745, with median compensation of $322,816.

4. Other compensation

About 2 percent of non-ODTKEs (in the Faculty and Heads of Departments categories) received compensation from a related organization averaging $86,432.

About 11 percent of non-ODTKEs received compensation averaging $207,257 that was reported as NCAA Athletic Income.[20] Most of these non-ODTKEs were Sports Coaches. About half of Sports Coaches received NCAA income, averaging $209,426, with median compensation of $15,550.

---

[20] For an explanation of NCAA Athletic Income, see Appendix C: Additional Data Analysis, Section V.C.

B. Compensation-Related Adjustments

Under section 4958, total compensation includes all items of compensation to determine reasonableness. The IRS examined compensation by looking at the gross income of individuals, generally assuming that all compensation in whatever form is taxable unless subject to a specific exception in the tax laws. This involved, among other things, analyzing whether fringe benefits and deferred compensation were properly excluded from wages. A wage adjustment could trigger a variety of taxes and penalties – for the individual liable for greater taxable income, for the institution liable for additional employment taxes and potentially for the individual and the institution should the adjustments resulted in an excess benefit transaction under section 4958.

The adjustments described below are not limited to ODTKEs and the highest-paid non-ODTKEs. The employment tax examinations covered all employees on payroll.

1. Wage adjustments

The IRS opened employment tax exams at 11 of the colleges and universities examined. All of the completed exams resulted in adjustments, amounting to increases in taxable wages of $35,540,808.98 and generating $7,076,387.22 in employment taxes (federal withholding, Social Security and Medicare) and $167,242.90 in penalties.

Wages were adjusted for a number of reasons:

- failure to include in income the value of the personal use of automobiles, housing, social club memberships and travel;[21]
- misclassification of employees as independent contractors;[22]
- failure to withhold taxes for wages paid to non-resident aliens;[23] and
- failure to include in income the value of certain graduate tuition waivers and reimbursements.[24]

---

[21] Inclusion of these amounts in the income of the disqualified persons who received these benefits did not result in excess benefit transactions. The benefits were not automatic excess benefit transactions under section 4958(c)(1)(A) because they were described in employment agreements, and the amounts involved did not render the disqualified persons' total compensation amounts unreasonable.

[22] When making payments to an employee (unlike when making payments to an independent contractor), an employer generally must withhold income taxes, withhold and pay Social Security and Medicare taxes, and pay unemployment tax on wages paid to an employee.

[23] Non-resident aliens are generally liable for Social Security and Medicare taxes on wages paid to them for services performed by them in the United States.

[24] In general, the tuition reduction benefit of section 117(d)(1) of the Code is limited to education below the graduate level, unless graduate students are engaged in teaching or research activities at an educational organization described in section 170(b)(1)(A)(ii).

2. Deferred compensation-related adjustments

The IRS opened retirement plan examinations at eight of the colleges and universities examined and found compliance issues at about half. Examinations resulted in deferred compensation-related wage adjustments on Forms 941 and 1040 of $1,115,007.00 generating $201,298.00 in taxes and $12,036.74 in penalties.

Wages were adjusted primarily for the following reasons:

- contributions that had to be taken into income in current years because the payments were not conditioned upon the future performance of substantial services sufficient to convey a substantial risk of forfeiture under section IRC 457(f)(3)(B).
- loans from 403(b) plans exceeded IRC 72(p) limits so that deemed distributions were included in gross income.
- deferrals for a 403(b) plan exceeded IRC 402(g) limits.
- additions to a 403(b) plan exceeded IRC 415(c) limits.

3. How Compensation Was Determined

Examinations looked at the process by which private colleges and universities set compensation. To a large extent, these institutions followed practices in setting compensation that are consistent with meeting the rebuttable presumption of reasonableness. In fact, the compensation of 94 percent of ODTKEs at examined colleges and universities was set using a procedure intended to satisfy the rebuttable presumption of section 4958.

Nearly two thirds had formal compensation policies in place that applied to at least one ODTKE in the years under examination. Of those ODTKEs who were not subject to a formal policy during the exam years, over half were covered by such a policy in subsequent years.[25]

Either the board of directors or the compensation committee of the board set compensation levels for each ODTKE. Compensation was set according to procedures designed to avoid conflicts of interest. The compensation of each ODTKE was approved in advance by individuals who did not have a conflict of interest. In almost every case, individuals recused themselves from discussions about their compensation. In nearly every case, the college or university documented the basis for setting compensation before the person received the compensation. Even when the engineers found the initial contract exception applied to compensation at examined colleges and universities, the

---

[25] Most examinations were for tax years ending in 2006, 2007 and 2008. The 2008 Form 990, Return of Organization Exempt From Income Tax, due in 2009, was the first time organizations were required to report information to the IRS about their compensation practices and policies.

institutions followed procedures that were consistent with the rebuttable presumption – i.e., they relied on comparability data to set the compensation level.[26]

About half of colleges and universities used an outside compensation consultant to assist with setting compensation levels, and about half did not. Current surveys of position-specific compensation paid by colleges and universities were the most commonly used tool for determining comparable compensation for each position, whether or not a compensation consultant was employed.

C. Reasonableness of compensation

LB&I Engineers evaluated compensation paid to ODTKEs at private colleges and universities under examination to evaluate whether compensation was reasonable within the meaning of section 4958. The Engineers issued reports scrutinizing the determinations involved in establishing the rebuttable presumption. They asked whether comparability data was truly comparable – specifically, was it based on similarly situated institutions and functionally comparable positions? Once they established comparable data, they determined where the compensation fell within the range of compensation (i.e., at which percentile).

1. Observations on weaknesses in comparability data

The engineers identified a number of weaknesses in the comparability data relied on by colleges and universities to establish the rebuttable presumption.

o About 20 percent of the private colleges and universities included institutions in their data set that were not similarly situated.[27] Engineers looked to factors such as: type (e.g., private or public; liberal arts, research university, etc.), size of undergraduate enrollment, faculty size, location (urban, rural, suburban; region of the US), endowment size, tuition and cost to attend, selectivity (SAT ranges, etc.) and age of the institution (year founded). The engineers found institutions were not comparable based on at least one of the following factors: location, endowment size, revenues, total net assets, number of students, and selectivity.

---

[26] Treas. Reg. § 53.4958- 4(a). Under the initial contract exception, compensation is not subject to section 4958 as long as it involves fixed payments made pursuant to that initial contract entered into before the individual became a disqualified person.

[27] Treas. Reg. § 53.4958-6(c)(2). An authorized body that has appropriate data as to comparability if, given the knowledge and expertise of its members, it has information sufficient to determine whether, the compensation arrangement in its entirety is reasonable. In the case of compensation, relevant information includes, but is not limited to, compensation levels paid by similarly situated organizations, both taxable and tax-exempt, for functionally comparable positions; the availability of similar services in the geographic area of the applicable tax-exempt organization; current compensation surveys compiled by independent firms; and actual written offers from similar institutions competing for the similar services.

- Compensation studies provided by the colleges and universities often did not document the selection criteria for the schools in the surveys provided and did not offer an explanation as to why those schools were deemed comparable to the school relying on the study and under examination.
- Many colleges and universities relied on a compensation survey compiled by an independent firm in which their compensation data was included. However, the survey itself was not limited to schools that were sufficiently similar to all be comparable to each other. Some used the survey results without any adjustment; others removed schools that they determined were not sufficiently comparable.
- Compensation surveys relied on for comparability data often did not specify whether amounts reported included only salary or included other types of compensation to equal total compensation, as required by section 4958.

The selection of schools used for comparison determines whether total compensation appears to be high or low. The same compensation amount might be in the 25th percentile among one set of schools, but in the 90th percentile among another. For most positions for which engineers modified the list of comparable schools, the compensation was pegged at a higher percentile in the comparable data sets created by the engineers than in the data relied upon by the examined college or university.

2. Other observations

Organizations are permitted to use amounts paid by taxable organizations as comparable data. The colleges and universities examined, however, did not rely on compensation paid by taxable organizations to set compensation. Some compensation consultants did provide for-profit comparability data alongside comparable data for exempt colleges and universities to further inform the compensation-setting body, but not to set compensation.

Moreover, only for one position, that of the chief investment officer did some institutions look to other types of exempt organizations for comparability data. Some examined colleges and universities with very large endowments relied on a survey that included compensation for the chief investment officer position at both colleges and universities and private foundations with similarly sized endowments.

After engineers either accepted the comparability data presented or established alternative comparability data, they determined where compensation paid by the examined organization fell within the range of compensation paid by colleges and universities in the comparable data set for each position. The compensation for most positions analyzed was set in the range of the 75th percentile. Moreover, compensation set at or above the 90th percentile was much more common than compensation set in the range of the 50th percentile among the examined colleges and universities.

III.   Outcomes of examinations

A. Written Advisories

The IRS issued written advisories to 24 institutions on a number of activities that could result in tax liability in the future. These advisories involved issues such as improper tracking of member types, characterization of income and expenses as related or unrelated, depreciation, attribution of expenses that are not primarily and proximately related to income and continuing losses that may indicate a lack of profit motive. They applied to activities including art galleries, hotels, conference centers, radio stations, parking lots, arenas and recreation centers.

B. Closures

Examinations have been closed at 31 of the 34 schools involving 117 separate Form 990-series returns, and the overwhelming majority of examinations closed with adjustments to returns.

SUMMARY OF ADDITIONAL DATA ANALYSIS

For the Final Report we have, where appropriate, weighted the Questionnaire responses to allow for the extrapolation of information from those organizations surveyed to all tax-exempt colleges and universities. This means that many of the findings apply not only to the particular respondents, but to the tax-exempt college and university sector as a whole.

In this section, we have summarized some of the questionnaire findings to present an overall picture of both the sector and the respondents. More detailed results and a greater discussion of the weighting of responses are available in Appendix C: Additional Data Analysis.

I.   Organization Information

- The average college and university in the fall of 2006:
  - o enrolled 3,800 full-time equivalent students.
  - o employed 1,700 individuals, including 200 full-time faculty members, 200 part-time adjunct faculty members, 600 students and 750 staff.
  - o had a student-faculty ratio of 13:1.
  - o charged annual in-state tuition of $12,600 and out-of-state tuition of $14,800.
  - o had gross assets of $361 million and net assets of $245 million.
  - o had gross revenue of $141 million and total expenses of $121 million with excess revenue of $20 million.
  - o maintained some form of off-site learning, with 63 percent conducting distance learning activities and 37 percent conducting educational programs outside the United States. Only 2 percent maintained offices, campuses and/or employees in at least five countries outside the United States.
  - o had endowment funds.

II.   Unrelated Business Activities

- About 60 percent of all colleges and universities had, at some point, filed a Form 990-T, with public institutions more likely than private to have filed.

- The activities most frequently reported on Form 990-T were Facility Rental (14 percent), Advertising (11 percent) and Recreation Center Usage (9 percent).

- All colleges and universities engaged in activities that they did not report on Form 990-T. Of the three most frequently reported activities (whether or not reported on Form 990-T):

- o 63 percent of colleges and universities engaged in Facility Rental with 14 percent reporting it on Form 990-T;

- o 54 percent engaged in Bookstore with 7 percent reporting it; and

- o 48 percent engaged in Food Service with 2 percent reporting it.

- The following shows by activity, the percentage of public and private colleges and universities engaged in that activity compared to the percentage reporting that activity on Form 990-T:

  - o Public

    - Facility rental, 82 percent engaged with 53 percent reporting.

    - Food services, 64 percent engaged with 5 percent reporting.

    - Bookstore, 60 percent engaged with 12 percent reporting.

  - o Private

    - Facility rental, 57 percent engaged with 11 percent reporting.

    - Bookstore, 52 percent engaged with 5 percent reporting.

    - Food services, 42 percent engaged with 1 percent reporting.

III. Endowment Funds

- 89 percent of all colleges and universities had endowment funds. 83 percent had endowment funds in their own name.

- 57 percent had another organization hold or maintain endowment funds on their behalf.

- 75 percent had an investment committee that oversaw investment of endowment funds, with an average of eight people on the investment committee.

- 64 percent engaged an outside consultant for investment guidance.

- 93 percent of the investment committees approved the selection of external parties used to manage the investments of endowment funds, while 83 percent approved investment-guidance recommendations made by outside consultants.

- For the fiscal year ending in 2006:

  - o the average amount of endowment assets per full-time equivalent student was $53,656;

  - o the average year-end fair market value of all endowment assets was $167 million;[28]

---

[28] This reflects questionnaire responses. As a result, the total endowment figure is less than the sum of the term, quasi and true endowment figures below.

- the average year-end fair market value of quasi endowments (i.e. unrestricted gifts) was $56 million;

- the average year-end fair market value of term endowments (i.e. those that can be spent after a term has passed) was $81 million; and

- the average year-end fair market value of true endowments (i.e. those where only the return on principal can be spent) was $82 million.

- 79 percent of investment committees or boards adopted a target spending rate for all endowments, which averaged 5 percent. 90 percent of those that adopted a target spending rate met the adopted rate.

- Of total endowment distribution, 56 percent were made for scholarships, awards, grants and/or loans in the amount of $3 million. 29 percent of total endowment distributions were made for general university operations in the amount of $3 million.

- 98 percent monitored endowment distributions to ensure that they were used for the donor's intended purpose(s). 86 percent monitored the distributions through reports; 54 percent monitored through financial audits on distributions.

IV.   Compensation Practices

- Executive Compensation
  - 35 percent had a formal written compensation policy that governed compensation of at least some officers, directors, trustees, or key employees.
  - 21 percent reported that they hired an outside executive compensation consultant to provide comparable compensation data to determine the compensation of officers, directors, trustees, or key employees. Of those, 37 percent had the executive compensation consultant provide other services.

- Compensation for officers was approved by:
  - Board of directors (66 percent)
  - Officers (31 percent)
  - Other individuals (21 percent)
  - Compensation committee (20 percent)

- Compensation for directors was approved by:
  - Other individuals (17 percent)
  - Board of directors (15 percent)
  - Officers (12 percent)
  - Compensation committee (3 percent)

- Compensation for key employees was approved by:
  - Officers (54 percent)
  - Board of directors (26 percent)
  - Other individuals (22 percent)
  - Compensation committee (11 percent)

V. Compensation Amounts

- The responses for compensation amounts were not weighted. As such, the information discussed below does not apply to colleges and universities overall.

- The information below describes the compensation for the group of individuals listed among the highest-paid officers, directors, trustees, and key employees (ODTKEs):

  - For each position — CEO/Chancellor/President, Executive Director, CFO, Treasurer/Vice President, and Dean — the average compensation paid by large colleges and universities was more than twice that paid by small, with the compensation paid by medium institutions falling in the middle. For example, average compensation for CEO/Chancellor/President was as follows:

    - Small: $197,952
    - Medium: $294,798
    - Large: $399,723

  - The total average compensation of the highest paid ODTKEs ranged from a low of $109,746 to a high of $399,723.

- The information below describes the compensation for the group of individuals listed among the six highest-paid non-ODTKEs:

  - The total average compensation of the highest paid non-ODTKEs ranged from a low of $90,651 to a high of $832,677.

  - Of the highest paid non-ODTKEs, Sports Coaches had the highest average and median compensation across all sizes of colleges and universities.

  - Of the highest-paid non-ODTKEs at colleges and universities in each of the size categories:

    - Small

      - 55 percent served primarily as Faculty (instructional and research) with average compensation of $129,663 and median compensation of $86,183;

      - 24 percent served primarily as Administrative/Managerial with average compensation of $90,651 and median compensation of $85,174;

- 17 percent served primarily as Head of Department with average compensation of $150,664 and median compensation of $94,068; and

- Fewer than 1 percent served primarily as Sports Coach with average compensation of $216,678 and median compensation of $95,162.

- Medium

  - 51 percent served primarily as Faculty (instructional and research) with average compensation of $185,529 and median compensation of $141,842;

  - 21 percent served primarily as Head of Department with average compensation of $187,944 and median compensation of $141,712;

  - 16 percent served primarily as Administrative/Managerial with average compensation of $173,117 and median compensation of $145,794; and

  - 6 percent served primarily as Sports Coach with average compensation of $326,802 and median compensation of $196,341.

- Large

  - 44 percent served primarily as Faculty (instructional and research) with average compensation of $346,490 and median compensation of $229,994;

  - 18 percent served primarily as Sports Coach with average compensation of $832,677 and median compensation of $485,781;

  - 16 percent served primarily as Head of Department with average compensation of $316,188 and median compensation of $205,363; and

  - 11 percent served primarily as Administrative/Managerial with average compensation of $217,131 and median compensation of $174,273.

APPENDIX A: Compliance Check Questionnaire

Questions and Answers

APPENDIX B: Interim Report

APPENDIX C: Additional Data Analysis

APPENDIX D: SYSTEMS

I. Introduction

Campuses of a university system were permitted to respond to the Questionnaire on a system-wide basis, rather than on a campus-only basis, if (1) system-wide reporting was consistent with reporting on Forms 990 and 990-T, and (2) the same method was used for all parts of the Questionnaire. Sixteen of the 400 colleges and universities that received a Questionnaire responded on a system-wide basis, identifying themselves as part of a total of six different systems.[29]

While the campuses were permitted to respond as systems, the sample and the Questionnaire were designed with campuses as the intended unit of analysis. Therefore, information provided on a system-wide basis was not included in the statistical analysis of survey responses presented in the Additional Data Analysis in Appendix C.

Readers should be careful not to draw conclusions regarding the information presented on systems in this Appendix D. The campuses that responded on a system-wide basis are not representative of the broader population of system-wide schools in the country. Furthermore, while respondents were instructed to answer all questions as systems if they answered any as systems, it is possible that respondents answered some questions for their individual campuses. The Questionnaire was written for individual campuses, and respondents may have answered some questions accordingly. As such, the information presented in this section cannot be used to draw conclusions for all university systems. This information is included for informational purposes only.

Unlike the presentation of information in the Additional Data Analysis, the discussion of the systems' responses includes limited raw data. A separate statistical analysis of systems' responses was not possible for the reasons discussed above. For most questions, narrative explanations are provided, but some could not be addressed because they would have required potentially misleading reporting of dollar figures.[30]

---

[29] The Interim Report reported that 11 campuses responded as part of a system. Further review indicates that 16 responded as part of a system.

[30] The following questions are not discussed with respect to systems: Questions 11 -12 (tuition), 13 (financial data), 17 (compensation), 46-67 (value of endowments and target spending rates), 48-50 (types of endowment funds), 75-94 (compensation policies and practices).

II.   Organization Information

A. General Observations of Systems

1. Overview

- The six systems discussed in this appendix consist of both private and public institutions.

- On average, the six systems had over 43,000 Full Time Equivalent (FTE) students with over 4,800 full-time faculty members, reporting an average student to faculty ratio of 19:1.

2. Conflict of Interest Policy and Public Disclosure of Audited Financial Statements (Questions 8 – 10)

- All systems had a written conflict of interest policy that governs members of their top management officials or ruling body, while most had one in place for their full-time faculty.

- All systems also made their audited financial statements available to the public.

3. International and Other Activities (Questions 14 – 16)

- All systems conducted long distance learning activities and most conduced educational programs outside of the United States.

- About half maintained some sort of international physical presence in the way of offices, campuses and/or employees in at least five countries outside the United States...

4. Related Organizations (Questions 18 – 19)

- All systems had at least one related organization, the most common of which was a tax-exempt organization.

- Roughly half of the systems reported at least one related organization that was taxable as a corporation or trust.

- Most of the systems had written policies, or some other process, in place to assure that transactions with non-501(c)(3) related organizations (whether taxable or exempt) are made at arm's length for any arrangement that deals with the provision of goods or services, lending money, property rental, and transfers of assets. In the other arrangements, only some of the systems established an arm's length process.

5. Controlling Organizations (Questions 20 and 22)

- Most systems defined themselves as a controlling organization within the meaning of IRC § 512(b) (13). Those systems that identified themselves as controlling organizations each controlled an average of about two entities.

III. ACTIVITIES

A. General Observations of Systems

1. Participation in Activities (Question 23)

- Of the potential activities, all systems universally engaged in only two activities: facility rental and food services.

- More than half of the systems also reported engaging in the following additional activities: advertising, particularly printed publications and tv/radio broadcasting; corporate sponsorships; certain royalties; patents, copyrights and trade names or trade secrets; parking lot commissions; bookstores; and activities other than those enumerated in the Questionnaire.

2. Unrelated Business Income Treatment (Questions 26 – 27)

- Half of all systems reported the following as unrelated business income activities: advertising, facility rentals, partnership allocations, bookstores and activities other than those enumerated in the Questionnaire.

3. Expense Allocations and Use of Outside Counsel (Questions 28, 30 and 31)

- Most systems indicated they had both direct and indirect expenses, with the direct expenses significantly outweighing the indirect expenses.

- Inter-company expenses, i.e., expenses paid or accrued to related organizations, accounted for a very small percentage of total expenses.

- Many of the systems relied on the advice of independent accountants or counsel for certain unrelated business issues for the 2006 tax year, particularly to determine whether activities were unrelated or exempt.

IV. ENDOWMENT FUNDS

A. General Observations of Systems

1. Endowment Funds and Management by Other Organizations (Questions 32 – 33)

- All six systems reported having endowment funds.

- Over half reported that they had another organization or institution that managed or maintained the endowment funds on their behalf.

2. Investment Policy and Fund Managers (Questions 34 – 35)

- All systems maintained an investment policy for endowment funds.

- All systems hired external party managers.

- For systems that indicated more than one type of fund manager type, in-house managers were the next commonly used type of fund manager.

3. Investment Committees, External Managers, Internal Managers and External Consultants (Questions 36 – 41)

- All systems had an investment committee that oversaw the investment of endowment funds.

- The average number of individual members on an investment committee overseeing the endowment funds was nine (the median number was twelve).

- The investment committees for most of the systems approved the selection of external investment managers for their endowment funds.

- The investment committees of all systems approved investment guidance recommendations made by outside consultants.

- The average number of staff individuals whose primary responsibility was investment management of endowments was five (the median was three).

- All systems engaged outside consultant for investment guidance.

4. Compensation to Fund Managers (Questions 42 – 45)
- Of the respondents that used internal investment managers, the primary source of compensation was wages or salary. Performance-based compensation was the next most common form.

- All systems compensated their external investment managers on asset-based fees. The next common forms of compensation included mutual fund fees and performance-based fees.

5. Value of Endowments and Target Spending Rate (Questions 46 – 47)
- At least half of the systems have a committee of the board or full board review and approve compensation for both their internal and external investment managers.

- All six systems had their investment committees adopt a target spending rate for all endowments, which averaged 4.0% with a median of 4.5%.

6. Life Income Funds (Question 51)
- Over half of the systems held in their endowments one or more of the listed life income funds (charitable gift annuities, charitable remainder trust and pooled income).

- Of those who responded to the second half of Q 51 in providing a percentage, those endowments consisted of small percentages of each type of life income fund.

7. Foreign Investments (Question 52)
- Many of the systems made foreign investments through an investment entity, which was most commonly formed as a corporation or partnership.

8. Investments (Questions 53 – 55)
- Every system invested in one or more type of equity and fixed income funds.
    - Only U.S. equity funds were in the investment portfolio of all six systems.

- Systems invested in both U.S. and non-U.S. equity and fixed income funds.

- Many systems' endowments also invested in alternative funds, such as private equity, hedge funds and venture capital funds. They also invested in real estate.

- Half of the systems held cash in their total investment pool.

- For all systems, the primary investment objective for their investment portfolio for the next five year period is a total real return (net of investment management fees) of 5% - 10%.

- A third of the systems reported that the board committee members of placed restrictions on the purchases or sales of certain securities due to particular donor restrictions or special requests.

9. **Distributions from Endowments (Questions 56 – 59)**
- All six systems distributed endowment funds for two categories: (1) scholarships, awards, grants and/or loans, and (2) general education support and/or libraries.

- All systems reported monitoring endowment distributions to ensure that the funds were used for the donor's intended purpose(s).

  - In order of common usage, the systems monitored the distributions with reports (monthly, quarterly or annual) and financial audits on distributions.

  - About half of the systems marked "other," and added such ways as campus departments and post-audit review procedures.

- All systems had a policy on disbursements made from endowments that were not used in the fiscal year of disbursement.

  - All reported applying undistributed amounts to the following year.

- Half also reported returning amounts to their endowment funds.

- Many of the systems also made distributions from endowments for the other categories, including: research, general university operations, chair positions and/or professorships, and other areas.

V. COMPENSATION

A. *General Observations of Systems*
1. **Compensation of Highest Paid Employees (Other than Officers, Directors, Trustees, or Key Employees) (Question 17)**
- Every system employed athletic coaches.

- Half of the systems reported that at least one of its five most highly paid employees received NCAA income.

2. Executive Compensation Amounts and Types of Remuneration (Questions 60 – 61)

- Very few systems reported that their highest-paid ODTKEs received compensation from related organizations.

- All six systems reported paying their highest paid individuals a base salary and providing contributions to employee benefit plans, such as health benefit.

- The next most common types of remuneration for these employees were contributions to life, disability and/or long-term care insurance, and providing housing and utilities.

- Half of the systems also paid a bonus, permitted personal use of the organization-owned or leased vehicles, and checked the box indicating other compensation (not otherwise classified).

- Systems also reported providing personal travel for the highly paid employee or a spouse, personal services (e.g. housekeeper, lawn service, etc.), expense reimbursements, health/social dues, other incentives or executive fringe benefits.

- Both employee and employer contributions are made to various deferred compensation plans.

  - Employees in most systems participate and contribute to deferred compensation plans under IRC 401(a), IRC 403(b), IRC 457(b).

  - Most systems also contribute to an IRC 401(a) plan.

  - A few systems also made contributions to IRC 403(b) and IRC 457(f) plans.

3. Executive Loans/Extensions of Credit (Questions 62 – 74)

- None of the systems provided loans or extended credit to their highest paid employees, including family members.

VI. GOVERNANCE
A. General Observations of Systems
1. Written Policies

- All systems reported having conflict of interest policies covering members of the ruling body and top management officials. Many also reported having conflict of interest policies covering full-time faculty.

- The number of systems that reported having conflict of interest policies or a statute in place to ensure specific transactions with related entities are made at arm's length varied.

  - Most of the systems had written policies or some kind of process in place to assure that transactions with non-501(c)(3) related organizations (taxable or exempt) are made at arm's length in arrangements that deal with the provision of goods or services, lending money, property rental, and transfers of assets.

- In the other arrangements, only some of the systems established an arm's length process.

- All six systems maintain an investment policy for endowment funds.

- All systems reported having a formal written policy that governed compensation of at least some of their officers, directors, trustees or key employees.

- Same respondents also reported having a written employment or independent contractor agreement with at least one of the six highest paid ODTKEs.

- None of the respondents reported providing executive loans to any of the six highest paid ODTKEs.

2. Public Disclosure of Financial Statements
- All six systems also make their audited financial statements currently available to the public.

3. Use of Outside Advisers
- Many of the systems relied on the advice of independent accountants or counsel for certain unrelated business issues for the 2006 tax year, particularly to determine whether activities were unrelated or exempt.

- All systems reported use of an external party to manage investments in the endowment fund, as well as for investment guidance.

4. Endowment Funds
- All systems had an investment committee to oversee their endowment fund.

- The average number of members on an investment committee that oversaw the endowment funds was nine (median number is 12).

- Investment committees of most of the systems approved the selection of external investment managers for their endowment funds.

- Investment committees of all systems approved investment guidance recommendations made by outside consultants.

- The average number of staff individuals whose primary responsibility was investment management of endowments was five (median is three).

- All systems engaged outside consultant for investment guidance.

- Some systems reported that the board or a committee placed restrictions on the purchase or sale of securities because of particular donor restrictions or requests.

- All systems reported monitoring endowment distributions to ensure that the funds were used for the donor's intended purpose(s).

5. Compensation

- Most systems reported that the board of directors or a compensation committee set compensation and that they used a process intended to satisfy the rebuttable presumption.

- All private systems also reported that the compensation of at least one of the six highest paid ODTKEs was approved by the board of directors or by another authorized governing body that did not have a conflict of interest.

- These same systems also reported that executives recused themselves from approving and voting on their own compensation.

- These systems also reported documenting the basis for setting the compensation of at least one of their six highest paid ODTKEs, as well as using an independent compensation comparability survey.